Simply Chopin

The Music of Frédéric Chopin
26 of His Most Loved Masterpieces

Arranged by Jerry Ray

D1601756

Simply Chopin is a collection of the most famous compositions by Frédéric Chopin (1810–1849), highlighting his mastery of writing for the piano. These pieces were carefully selected and arranged by Jerry Ray for Easy Piano, making many of Chopin's most beautiful melodies accessible to pianists of all ages. Phrase markings, articulations, fingering and dynamics have been included to aid with interpretation, and a large print size makes the notation easy to read.

Frédéric Chopin lived in the early 19th century during the Romantic period of music history. Chopin was a great innovator in writing solo pieces for small audiences outside of the concert hall. He perfected waltzes, mazurkas, nocturnes and polonaises. Chopin's greatest contribution to music was developing the piano as a solo instrument, unleashing its ability to "sing" with new pedal effects and its ability to dazzle with brilliant virtuoso passagework. In spite of this, the heart of Chopin's music lies in its soul; he was a superb craftsman but will be forever a poet. For these reasons and more, his compositions are exciting to explore.

After all, he is *Simply Chopin!*

Contents

Berceuse, Op. 57

(originally in the key of D-flat Major)

Frédéric Chopin
Arranged by Jerry Ray

Ballade No. 1 in G Minor, Op. 23

Frédéric Chopin
Arranged by Jerry Ray

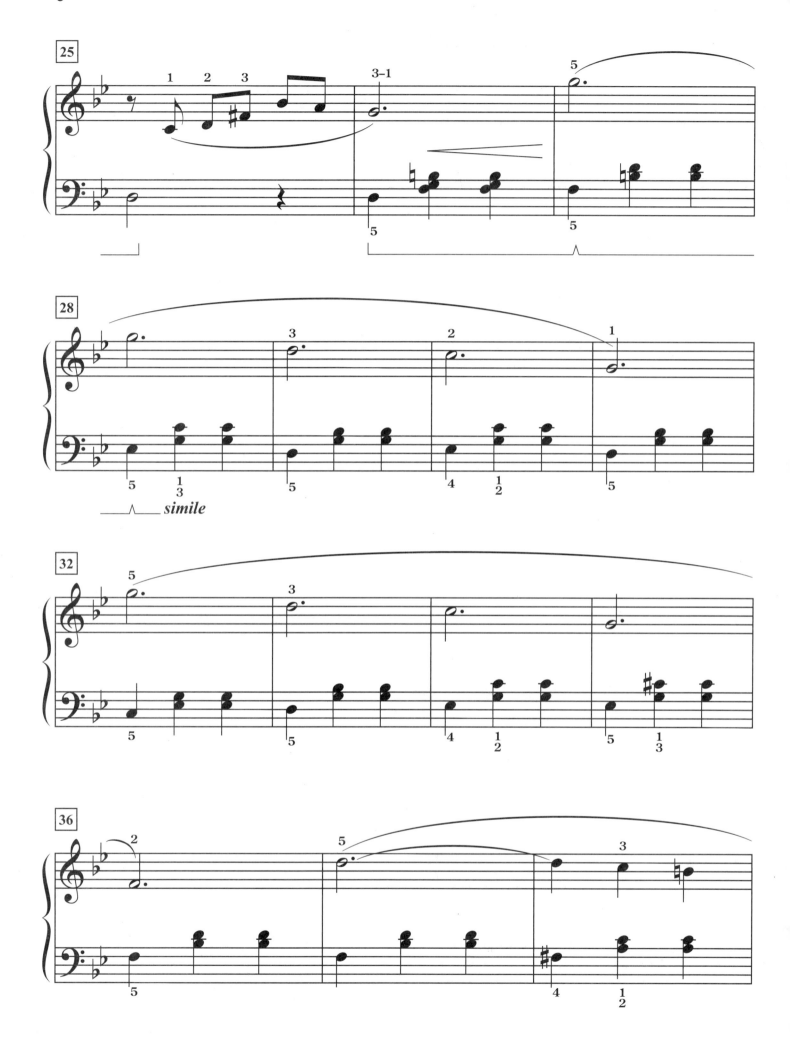

Etude, Op. 10, No. 3

(originally in the key of E Major)

Frédéric Chopin
Arranged by Jerry Ray

Fantaisie-Impromptu, Op. 66

(originally in the key of D-flat Major)

Frédéric Chopin
Arranged by Jerry Ray

Moderato cantabile

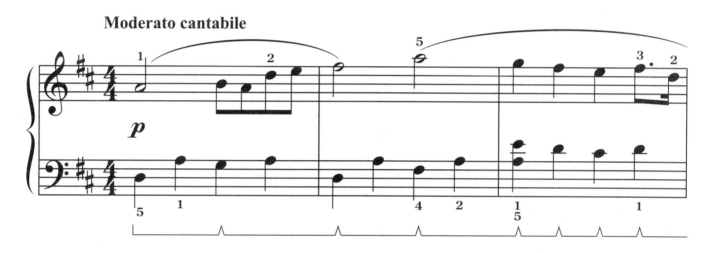

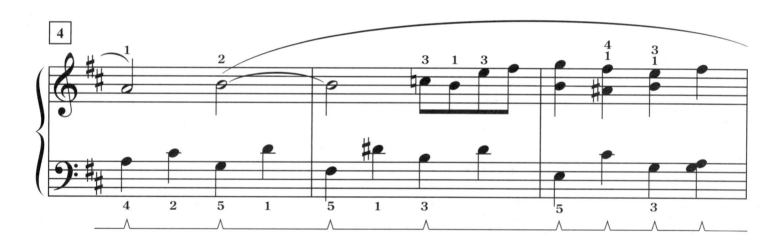

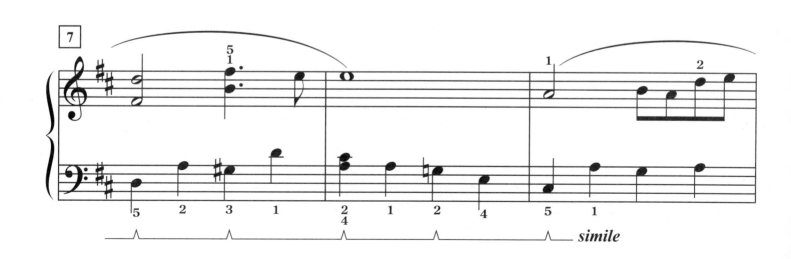

12

13

Etude in C Minor, Op. 10, No. 12

Revolutionary Etude

Frédéric Chopin
Arranged by Jerry Ray

Allegro con fuoco

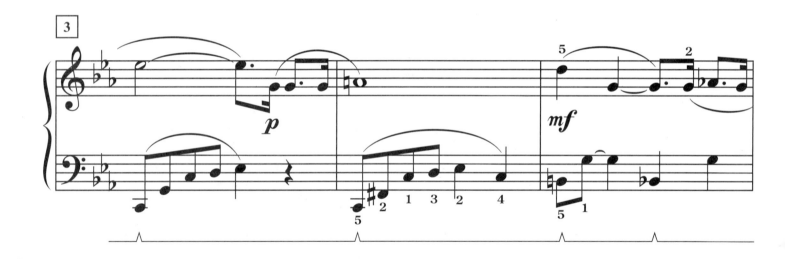

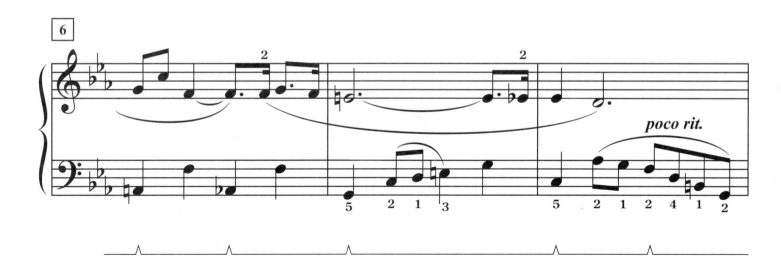

Grande Valse brillante
in E-flat Major, Op. 18

Frédéric Chopin
Arranged by Jerry Ray

Mazurka in G Minor, Op. 67, No. 2

Frédéric Chopin
Arranged by Jerry Ray

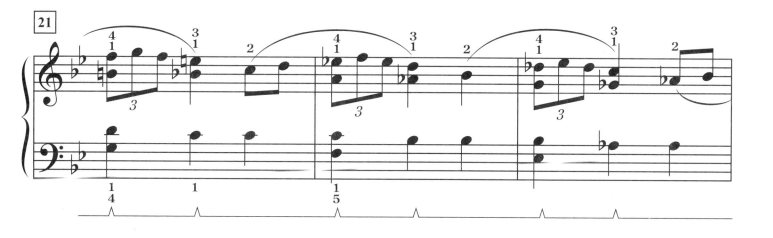

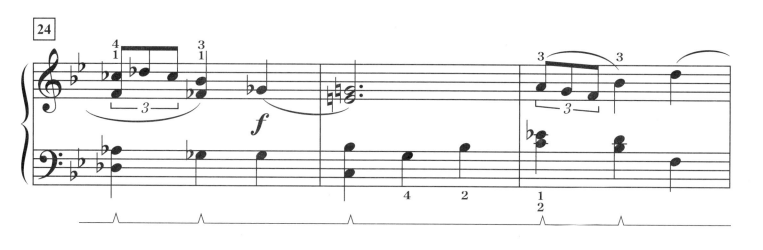

Mazurka in A Minor, Op. 67, No. 4

Frédéric Chopin
Arranged by Jerry Ray

Moderato animato

D.S. al Fine

Mazurka, Op. 24, No. 3

(originally in the key of A-flat Major)

Frédéric Chopin
Arranged by Jerry Ray

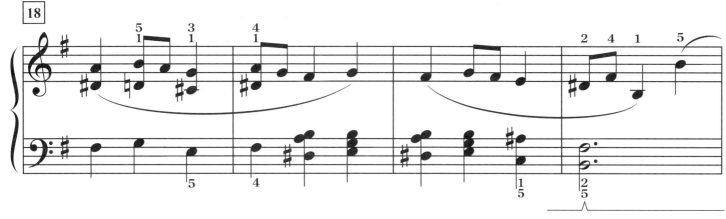

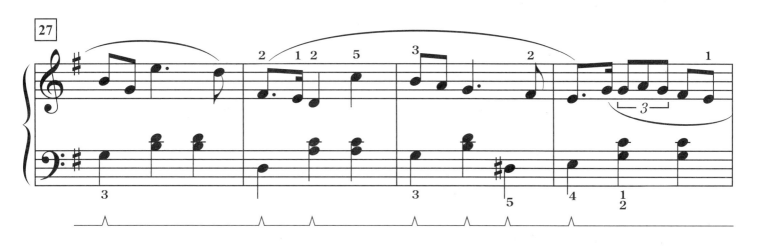

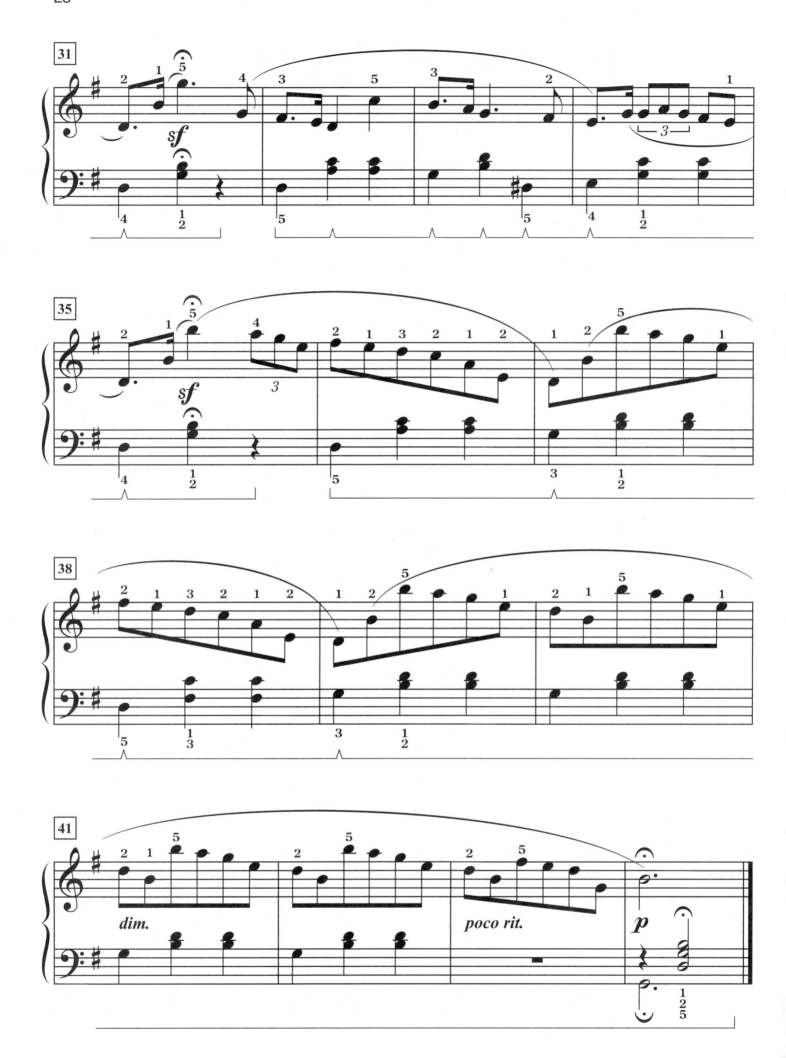

Nocturne in E-flat Major
Op. 9, No. 2

Frédéric Chopin
Arranged by Jerry Ray

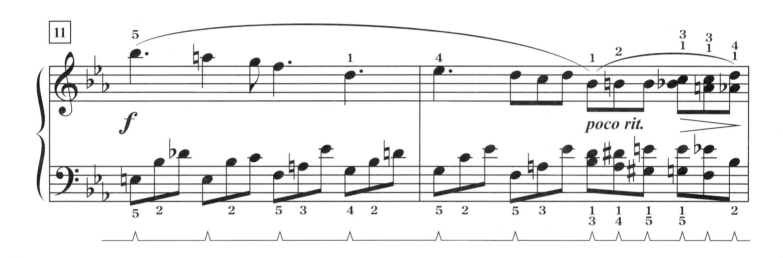

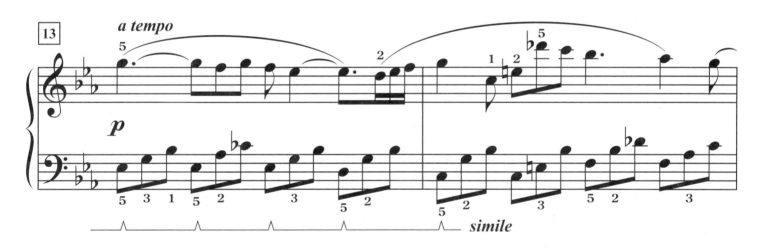

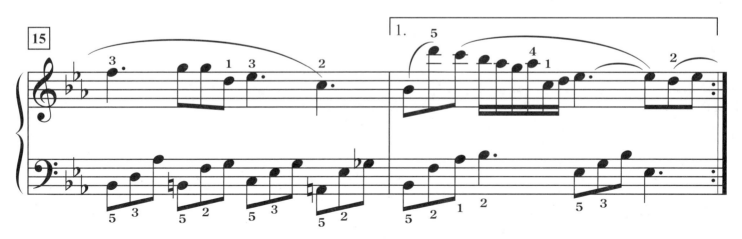

Nocturne, Op. 55, No. 1

(originally in the key of F Minor)

Frédéric Chopin
Arranged by Jerry Ray

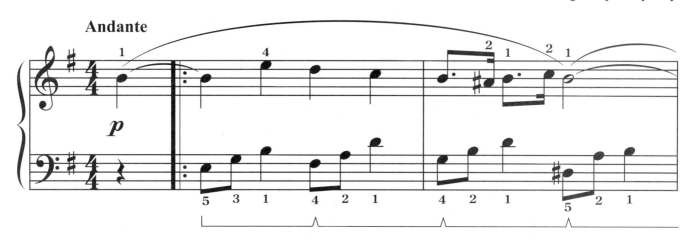

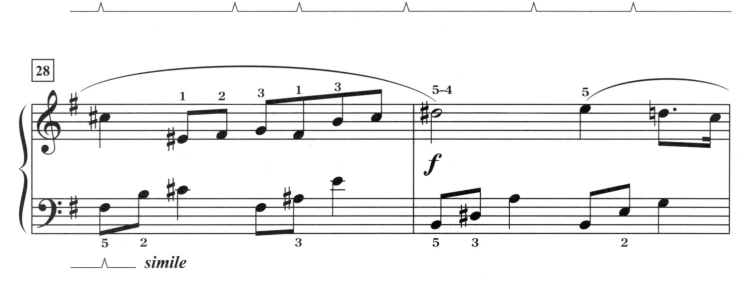

Piano Sonata No. 3, Op. 58

(First Movement)
(originally in the key of D Major)

Frédéric Chopin
Arranged by Jerry Ray

Allegro maestoso

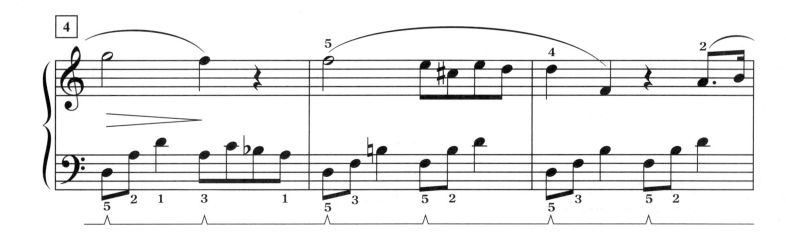

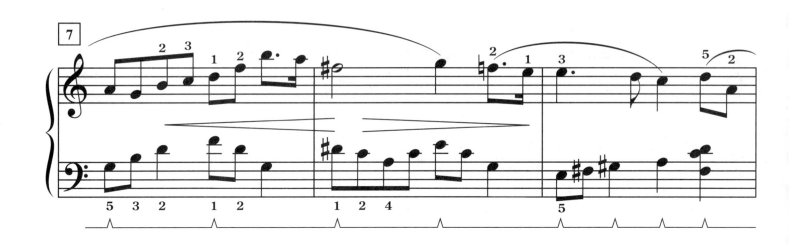

Piano Sonata No. 2, Op. 35

Funeral March

(Third Movement)

Frédéric Chopin
Arranged by Jerry Ray

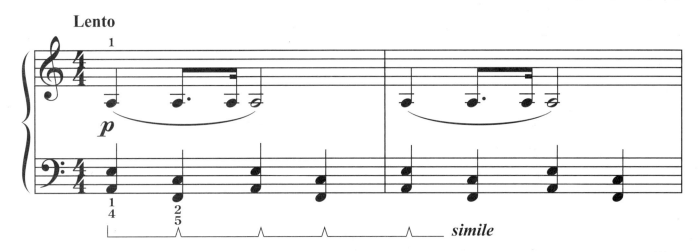

Polonaise, Op. 40, No. 1

Military Polonaise

(originally in the key of A Major)

Frédéric Chopin
Arranged by Jerry Ray

Allegro con brio

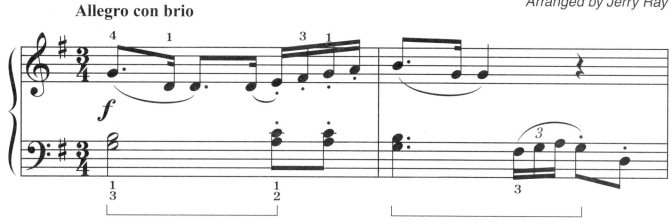

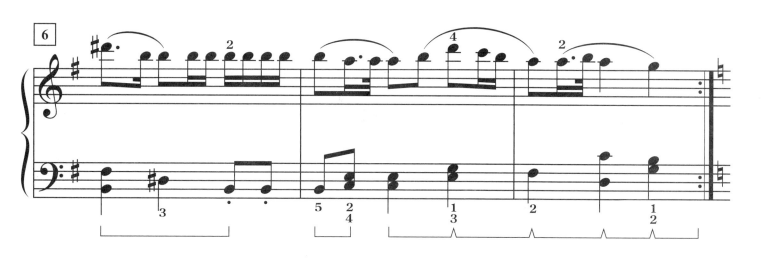

Polonaise, Op. 53

Heroic Polonaise

(originally in the key of A-flat Major)

Frédéric Chopin
Arranged by Jerry Ray

Prelude in A Major, Op. 28, No. 7

Frédéric Chopin
Arranged by Jerry Ray

Prelude in C Minor, Op. 28, No. 20

Frédéric Chopin
Arranged by Jerry Ray

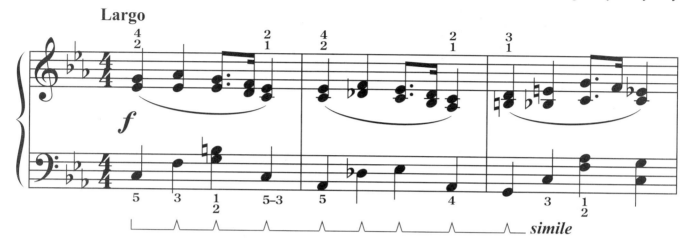

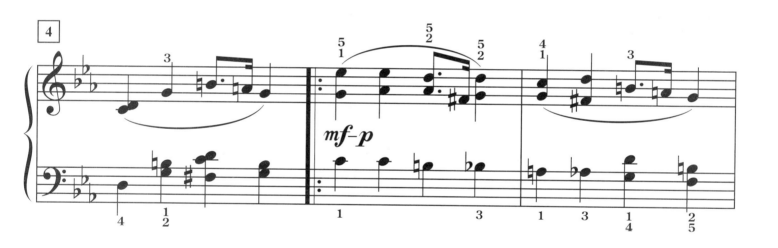

Prelude, Op. 28, No. 15

Raindrop Prelude

(originally in the key of D-flat Major)

Frédéric Chopin
Arranged by Jerry Ray

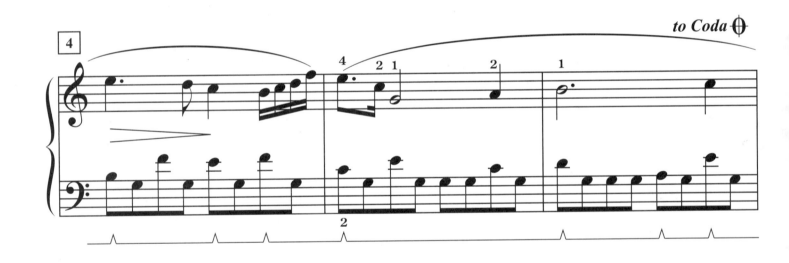

Prelude in E Minor, Op. 28, No. 4

Frédéric Chopin
Arranged by Jerry Ray

Valse brillante
in A Minor, Op. 34, No. 2

Frédéric Chopin
Arranged by Jerry Ray

Valse brillante, Op. 34, No. 1

(originally in the key of A-flat Major)

Frédéric Chopin
Arranged by Jerry Ray

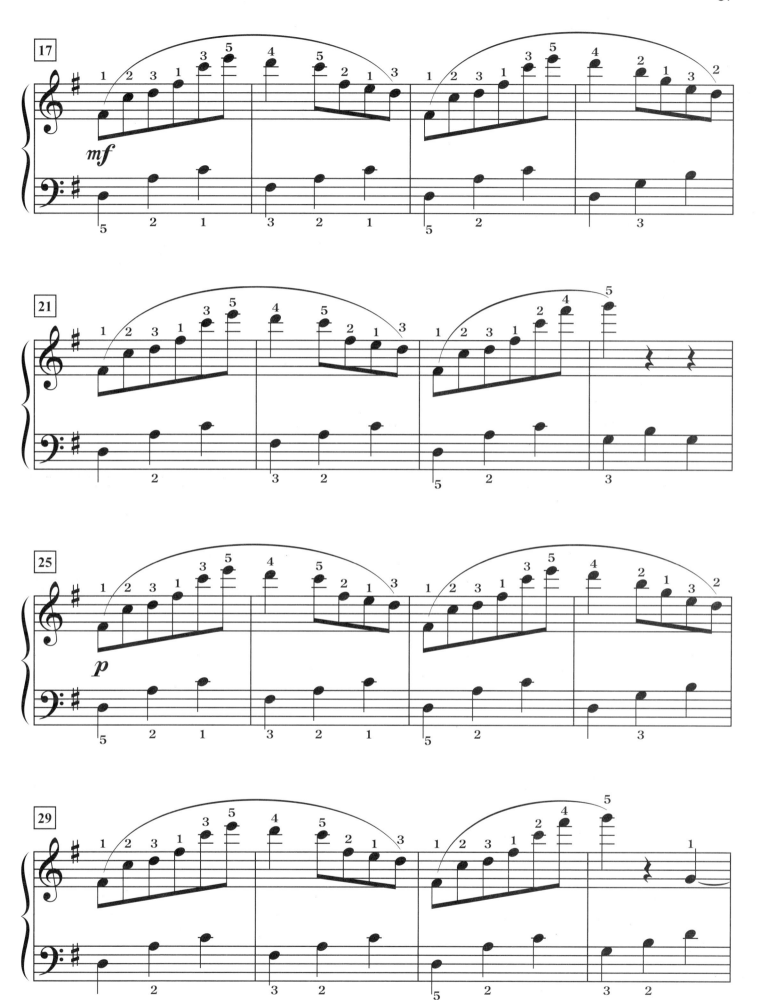

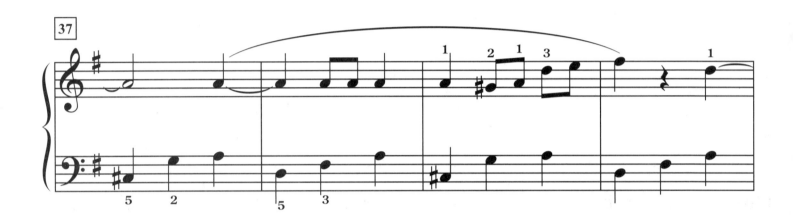

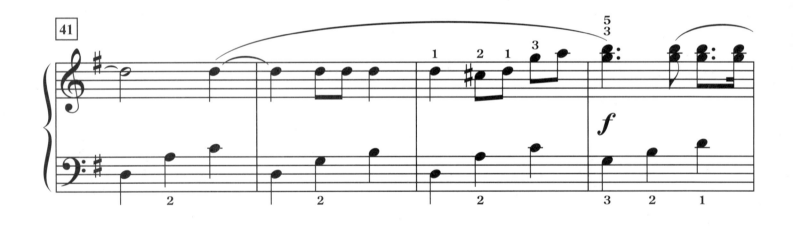

Waltz, Op. 64, No. 1

Minute Waltz

(originally in the key of D-flat Major)

Frédéric Chopin
Arranged by Jerry Ray

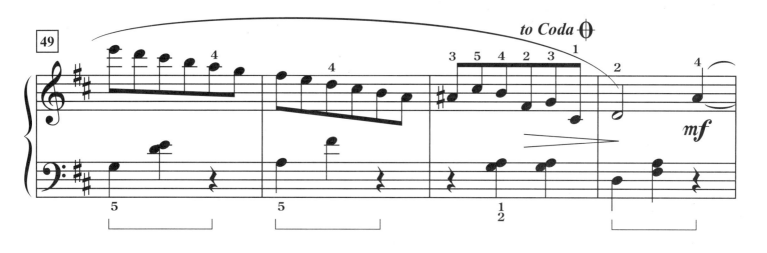

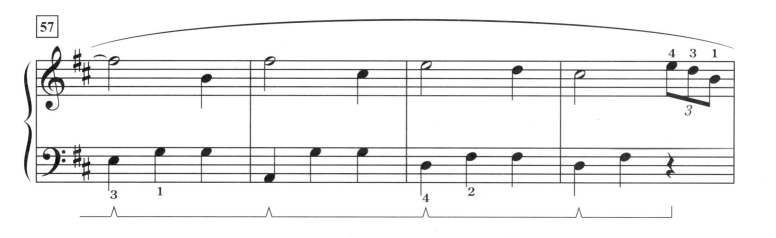

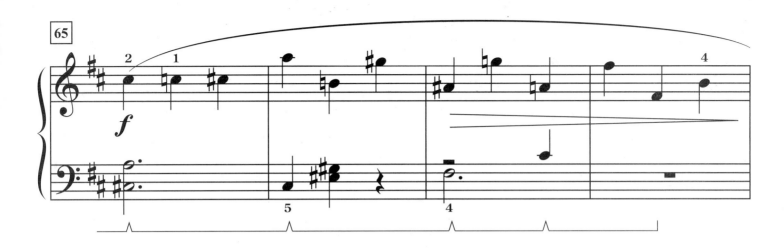

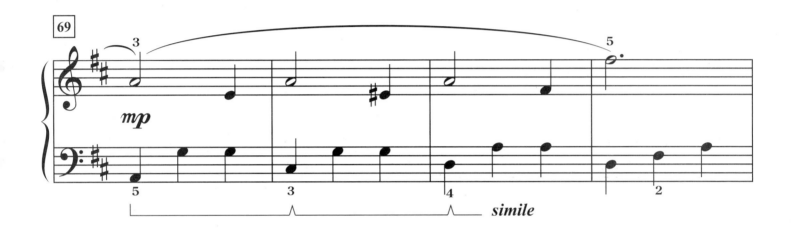

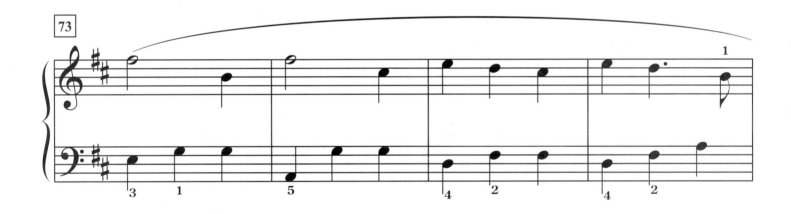

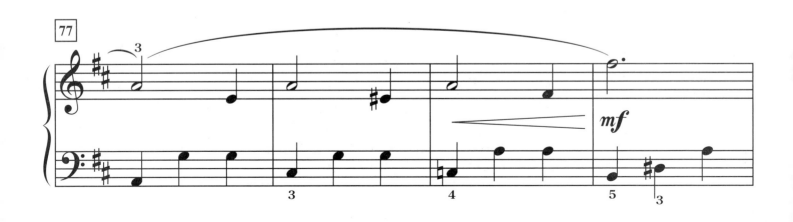

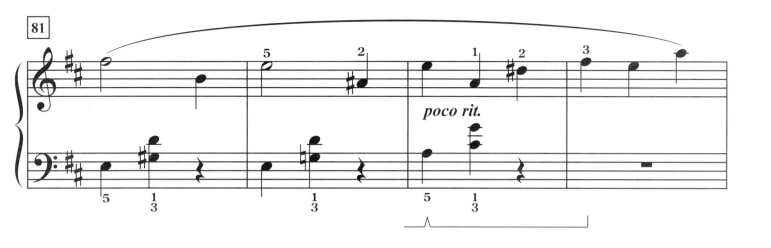

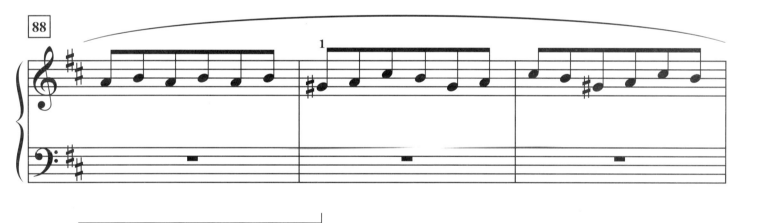

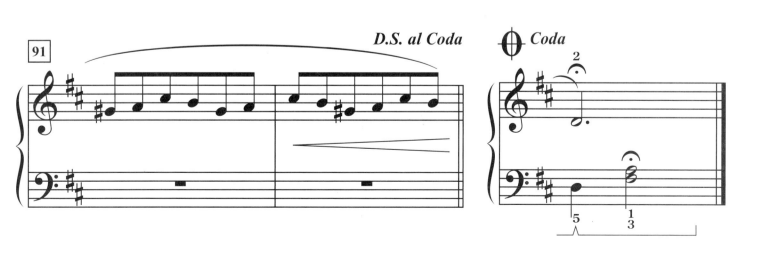

Waltz, Op. 64, No. 2

(originally in the key of C-sharp Minor)

Frédéric Chopin
Arranged by Jerry Ray

Waltz, Op. 69, No. 1

(originally in the key of A-flat Major)

Frédéric Chopin
Arranged by Jerry Ray

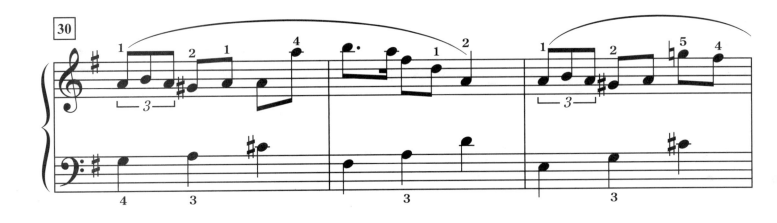

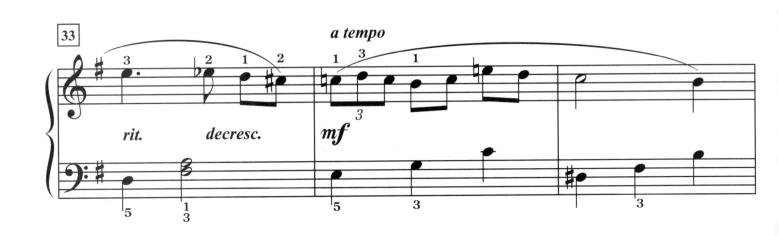

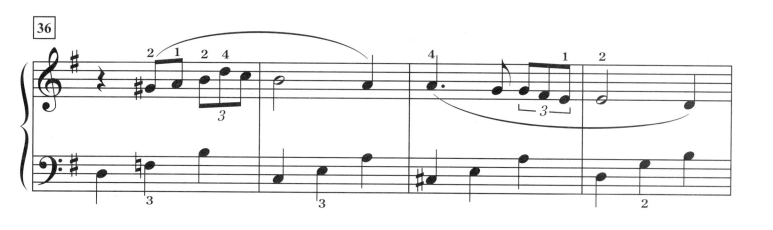
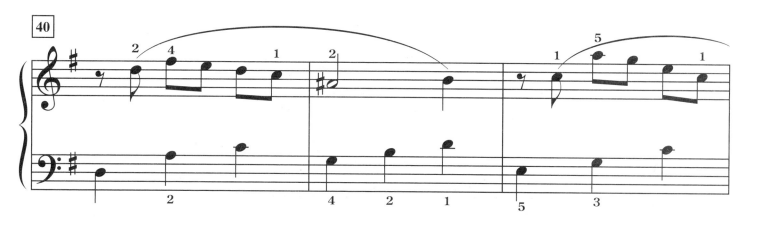

Waltz in E Minor

(Posthumous)

Frédéric Chopin
Arranged by Jerry Ray